When JESUS Sets You Free
You are Free Indeed

John P. McTernan, Chaplain

WWW.DEFENDERPUBLISHING.COM

When Jesus Sets You Free
You are Free Indeed
by John P. McTernan, Chaplain

Printed in the United States of America

ISBN 978-0-9904974-7-9

www.defenderpublishing.com

ADDITIONAL BOOKS
BY JOHN P. MCTERNAN, PhD

Books
As America Has Done to Israel
Israel: The Blessing or the Curse
God's Final Warning to America
Only Jesus of Nazareth Can Be Israel's King Messiah
Only Jesus of Nazareth Can Sit on the Throne of David
Only Jesus of Nazareth Can Be The God of Israel's Righteous Servant
I Could Take His Punch

Brochures
Only Jesus Christ Can Heal the Brokenhearted
The 666 Surveillance System

Blogs
John McTernan's Insights
The 666 Surveillance System
The Image of the Beast
God's Health System

John can be reached at: McT911@aol.com.
His website and blogs: USAProphecy.com
You can write to: PO Box 444, Liverpool, PA 17045

TABLE OF CONTENTS

LIST OF ILLUSTRATIONS

Badge: John P. McTernan

Scroll: Do You Know Your Divine Rights? By John P. McTernan

Federal Court Room Scene: ©iStock.com/JPLDesigns

Ten Commandments: ©iStock.com/duckycards

Marantz Recorder: By John P. McTernan

Picture of U.S. Supreme Court Building: @iStock.com/ bluestocking

Drawing of Jesus Christ on Cross: Created by Scaranoarts.com

Picture of Gavel: @kelpfish/dreamstime.com

Picture of U.S. Supreme Court Justices: @iStock. com/EdStock

Picture of man behind bars: @iStock.com/Mfpar35

Picture of man handcuffed: @jinga80/dreamstime.com

Picture of open handcuffs: @iStock.com/jgroup

Picture of broken leg: @iStock.com/joloei

Picture of healed leg: @iStock.com/ntdanai

Endorsement

"The LORD looseth the prisoners"
(Psalms 146:7)

In 1981 when I founded the PMI Center for Biblical Studies there were less than 500,000 inmates occupying prison cells in America. That one-half million has now exploded into 2.2 million all crammed into dangerously overcrowded understaffed institutions that are nothing more than seamy cesspools of cultural debauchery. Consider this:

-American penitentiaries are breeding grounds for the concentrated forces of evil that rule them!

-85% or more of America's prisoners have no relationship with Jesus Christ and fall prey to the rulers, gangs, sodomites, and Muslims who exploit them!

-Sodomy is occurring more frequently amongst professing Christian prisoners!

-Prison rehabilitation is a $60 billion dollar industry scam! It manufactures no products and ignores the core problem: humans are born with an empty place in their hearts that only God can fill.

-Of the 95% of prisoners that will one day be released, 75% will be back in prison within 48 months!

So what can we do to change this?

My friend Dr. John McTernan is a retired federal agent who is not only well versed in the depravity associated with America's justice system, but possesses acumen for linking together man's problems to Biblical solutions. I'm happy to say Dr. John recently released a timely new work called *When Jesus Sets You Free* where he masterfully correlates America's legal system with God's while taking careful aim at the source of the problem. His thesis is as simple as it is Biblical:

-We are all guilty criminals (sinners) sentenced to die for our crimes.

-There are millions locked away in brick and mortar penitentiaries, while others of us are imprisoned by broken hearts.

-Jesus Christ was arrested, imprisoned, tried, and sentenced to die for our crimes.

-Jesus Christ is also our defense attorney which rigs the outcome of the trial in our favor.

-Anyone regardless of their "criminal history" can call on Christ to receive complete forgiveness for their sins and healing for their broken heart.

All and all this is a great read and while there is so much more I could have included here, I urge you to obtain a copy of this insightful and touching book to read and share with someone who is either locked up in a government prison or one of their own mind.

Dr. Mike Johnston

Dr. Mike has been involved in jail and prison ministry since 1975. In 1981 he founded the PMI Center for Biblical Studies, to evangelize, educate, and equip prisoners for ministry. Since that time, he has enrolled and or trained over 20,000 inmates. Dr. Mike has served in a variety of ministries as an evangelist, pastor and teacher. He is the author of dozens of books and booklets, including PMI Center curriculum, collateral studies, treatises and tracts. He can be reached at: PmiMinistries.com

Preface

My Badge 5080

When I was a federal agent, I vividly remember arresting a young "businessman" for paying bribes to government officials. He owned and operated a massage parlor/bordello.

This was the first time that he had been arrested and he was frightened. He never had considered that he could be arrested and go to jail for his crimes. But the government had overwhelming evidence to convict him, including recorded conversations of him paying bribes.

After the arrest I searched him and found a laminated card with Psalm 23 on one side, and on the other, the Lord's Prayer. I held the card and looked right at him. He said that his parents were Christians and had given it to him. They had pleaded with him to come to Jesus Christ and get out of his life of crime. I told him, "You should have listened to them, because now you are in the hands of the U.S. Attorney." This young man was in intense fear. I saw it in his eyes, and heard it in his voice.

By the time that he had been processed, it was late in the day. I had to turn him over to the U.S. Marshals for an overnight stay in jail and arraignment before a judge the next day. As we walked to the Marshal's Office, his fear was turning into terror. I placed the laminated card in his shirt pocket and told him to read it, repent and turn to Christ.

The marshals knew we were coming, and two of them were waiting for us. When he saw them, the young man actually pleaded with me not to leave him. I told him that he had to face this alone. I stood and watched as the marshals grasped his arms and took him through metal doors into a holding cell. The young man looked back and we locked eyes. He was in sheer terror. In my mind, I still can see those eyes. They showed the fear that man's legal system can inflict on a person. But this terror is insignificant compared to what will happen when a person faces God from the wrong side of His divine legal system.

This book shows you how to be on the correct side of God's law and thus, never face the spiritual equivalent of the terror which that young man experienced for breaking man's law. Because God provided Jesus Christ as your Advocate, you can have assurance of forgiveness for your sins before God's court of justice.

The concepts in this book have resulted from a merger of my 26 years of career experience as a federal agent, my intensive study of the Bible, and my ministry to prisoners. All three merged in my mind to give me a very clear understanding of how God deals with man through a precise legal system. If you understand man's legal system, then it is very easy to understand God's. The key is to see sin as the equivalent of crime in God's system, and then all the rest falls into place.

May God use this book to give you assurance of eternal life with Him, through His ordained Advocate for you, Jesus Christ.

> 1 John 2:1 My little children, these things write I unto you, that ye sin not. And if any man sin, we have an advocate with the Father, Jesus Christ the righteous:

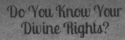

Do You Know Your Divine Rights?

You have the right to confess you are a sinner and have broken God's law. Romans 3:23 Do you understand?

You have the right to know, if you do not receive eternal salvation through Jesus Christ, every word you have spoken will be used against you on Judgment Day. Matthew 12:36,37 Do you understand?

You have the right to consult the Holy Bible to ensure you are being told the truth. Acts 17:11 Do you understand?

You have the right as a sinner to receive Jesus Christ as your Lord and Attorney, to defend you before the Divine Court of Law. 1 John 2:1 This will ensure you are acquitted of sin, and have eternal life with God. John 10:28 Do you understand?

You have the right at any time to stop this preaching and repent of your sins, and to confess Jesus Christ as your Lord and Attorney. Romans 10:9,10 If you do not confess Christ, you will be convicted of sin before the Divine Court of Law and face an eternal sentence in hell. Revelation 20:12-15 Do you understand?

CHAPTER ONE

GOD'S GREAT WHITE THRONE JUDGMENT AND HOW TO ESCAPE IT

> And I saw a great white throne, and him that sat on it ... And I saw the dead, small and great, stand before God; and the books were opened: and another book was opened, which is the book of life: and the dead were judged out of those things which were written in the books, according to their works ... And whosoever was not found written in the book of life was cast into the lake of fire. Revelation 20:11-15

The Great White Throne Judgment/Trial

I clearly remember many years ago, being a young federal agent sitting in the Eastern District of New York, Federal Court waiting for a pre-trial hearing. Sitting next to me on the left was the Assistant United States Attorney (AUSA) assigned to my case. The courtroom was very crowded, and I was daydreaming while I waited for the judge to call my case.

Suddenly, the AUSA elbowed me and pointed to an attorney who just had walked in front of me. He recognized the attorney as one who had represented a defendant in a recent case he had tried. He mentioned that the attorney was from a very prestigious law firm which had offices throughout America. The AUSA now became very interested in this case and so did I.

Following the attorney was a young female about 25 years old, and following her was a second attorney. The AUSA turned to me and after pointing out the second attorney, said that the defendant must be extremely wealthy. I was seated in the front row and could both see and hear everything that happened clearly.

I looked very carefully at the young woman, and noticed that she was very well dressed. She gave the appearance of being wealthy. The court called her name, and she approached the judge, who then spoke to her. He was dressed in a black robe and seated behind a high, impressive looking solid-wood desk. Directly behind the judge was a huge marble slab with the Seal of the United States in the middle. There was also a large American flag behind him. I glanced around at the majestic layout of the courtroom. The room appeared rich with solid-oak benches, tables, and chairs; even the walls had beautiful, solid-wood paneling.

The judge then read the charge against the woman. My eyes were riveted on her. She was charged with smuggling heroin into the United States. He asked if she understood the charge and how she pleaded. This obviously wealthy woman, flanked by two of the best attorneys that money could buy, bowed her head and, with a very weak voice that I could barely hear, said, "Guilty." Immediately, from the row behind me I heard crying and sobbing. I turned and there were her father and mother, and it was obvious from their dress that they were very wealthy.

I turned toward the judge and a second defendant's name was called. She was not well-dressed and looked poor. Standing next to her was a single attorney. Because she was a co-conspirator, the same charge was read to her. She then bowed her head and pleaded guilty also. Immediately to my right, I heard more crying and sobbing. I turned and looked at an entire row of people crying. They were this defendant's family. It was obvious from their dress that they were poor.

FEDERAL COURTROOM, SHOWING ITS GRANDEUR

In the midst of all this courtroom grandeur and authority, their crying and sobbing could be heard as both the rich and the poor made guilty pleas. No one could help them, not even lawyers from a prestigious law firm. Each had to answer alone to the judge for their crimes.

At this point, in the midst of the head-bowed guilty pleas, as I heard the cries of loved ones and gazed at the majesty of the courtroom surroundings, the Great White

Throne Judgment flashed into my mind. The events that just had transpired became clear, and I understood that this court resembled God's court! I realized that God deals with man through a legal system, a Divine legal system. This event permanently burned into my memory.

There is not a more ominous section in the entire Bible than Revelation, chapter 20. In this chapter, God is sitting on His Great White Throne during Judgment Day. Everyone who dies without Jesus Christ as Savior will face judgment before a holy, righteous and just God sitting on this throne. Each will have to answer alone, directly to God for his sin, just as the two women did in federal court.

In my position as a criminal investigator with the federal government, I had the privilege to witness the entire legal procedure from the beginning of an investigation when raw information was received, to a final U.S. Court of Appeals ruling on the case. With my legal background in mind I researched the Bible, and found that sure enough, the U.S. legal system parallels God's system.

The Gospel of Jesus Christ does not "hang in the air," but is tied directly into a Divine legal system. It is clear that God deals with man in a strict legal sense, which could one day end in your court appearance before the Great White Throne to stand trial for all of your sin.

God's Legal System Follows:

God's penal code: The Ten Commandments and the Sermon on the Mount. (Even thoughts are covered by this code!)

I THOU SHALT HAVE NO OTHER GODS BEFORE ME

II THOU SHALT NOT MAKE UNTO THEE ANY GRAVEN IMAGE

III THOU SHALT NOT TAKE THE NAME OF THE LORD THY GOD IN VAIN

IV REMEMBER THE SABBATH DAY, TO KEEP IT HOLY

V HONOUR THY FATHER AND THY MOTHER

VI THOU SHALT NOT KILL

VII THOU SHALT NOT COMMIT ADULTERY

VIII THOU SHALT NOT STEAL

IX THOU SHALT NOT BEAR FALSE WITNESS AGAINST THY NEIGHBOUR

X THOU SHALT NOT COVET

Exodus 20:3-17 Thou shalt have no other gods before me.

Thou shalt not make unto thee any graven image ...
Thou shalt not take the name of the LORD thy God in vain; for the LORD will not hold him guiltless that taketh his name in vain.
Remember the sabbath day, to keep it holy. But the seventh day is the sabbath of the LORD thy God: in it thou shalt not do any work ...
Honour thy father and thy mother: that thy days may be long upon the land which the LORD thy God giveth thee.
Thou shalt not kill.
Thou shalt not commit adultery.
Thou shalt not steal.

23

Thou shalt not bear false witness against thy neighbour.

Thou shalt not covet thy neighbour's house, thou shalt not covet thy neighbour's wife, nor his manservant, nor his maidservant, nor his ox, nor his ass, nor any thing that is thy neighbour's.

Matthew 5:28 Whosoever looks on a woman to lust after her has committed adultery with her already in his heart.

Purpose of God's penal code: To show guilt.

Deuteronomy 31:26 (speaking of the law) That it [the law] might be a witness against you.

Sin: A criminal act (felony) against the law:

1 John 3:4 Whosoever commits sin transgresses also the law for sin is the transgression of the law.

Romans 3:23 For all have sinned, and come short of the glory of God.

Evidence: Your own acts and words.

Matthew 12:36,37 Every idle word that men speak they shall give account thereof in the day of judgment. For by your words you shall be justified, and by your words you shall be condemned.

Trial: God's Great White Throne.

> Revelation 20:11-13 And I saw a great white throne, and him that sat on it ... And I saw the dead, small and great, stand before God; and the books were opened: and another book was opened, which is the book of life: and the dead were judged out of those things which were written in the books ... and they were judged every man according to their works.

Punishment: Jail, separation from God in hell.

> Revelation 20:14 And death and hell were cast into the lake of fire. This is the second death. (15) And whosoever was not found written in the book of life was cast into the lake of fire.

Jail Sentence Duration: Eternity.

> Matthew 25:41 Depart from me, you cursed into the everlasting fire.

This legal system is so detailed that there are both prosecuting and defense attorneys! The Bible states that satan is the accuser of the believers (Revelation 12:10), while Jesus Christ is our court appointed advocate or defense attorney!

1 John 2:1 We have an advocate with the Father, Jesus Christ the righteous.

Incriminating Evidence Presented at the Great White Throne Trial

Today, through the use of sophisticated electronic devices, law enforcement can monitor and record conversations (words). These words then can be produced in court at a future date as evidence to convict a defendant. This exactly parallels what the Bible says about God's legal system. God will use people's words to convict them before His court.

> Matthew 12:36,37 But I say to you that every idle word that men shall speak, they shall give account thereof on the day of judgment. For by your words you shall be justified and by your words you shall be condemned.

The following is an actual investigation and court trial of mine, which took place in the Eastern District of New York (Long Island). It shows how closely human government parallels God's legal system. By understanding how law enforcement operates, you can understand how God's government functions.

I received information from the local police regarding a leading organized crime (OC) member, Joe, who was operating in Long Island. He was involved with loan sharking, murder, and union racketeering. Joe had attacked his girlfriend's vehicle with a baseball bat while she was sitting in it. She was terrified and went to the local police for help.

The girlfriend provided police with significant information about Joe's criminal activity, including where he had hidden both money and assets. She also told them that Joe recently had been audited and had paid a bribe to a federal agent. But when she learned that the police could not immediately arrest Joe, she refused to cooperate. Without her, the police could not continue the investigation, so they contacted me with her information. I researched IRS records and found that Joe had been audited recently, with no change to his taxes.

I initiated a new audit with an undercover revenue agent. The agent was wearing a body recorder, and all of the meetings and telephone calls were recorded, and numerous pictures were taken of the meetings. The undercover agent used the information obtained from Joe's girlfriend to press his accountant for records. The accountant then offered the agent a $5000 bribe to stop the audit without a tax increase, and the agent agreed.

After making arrangements to pay the bribe, the accountant contacted the undercover agent and requested an urgent meeting. During this meeting, the accountant said that Joe had hidden a huge amount of unreported income, which would result in a significant amount of additional taxes. The accountant said that he had told Joe that the amount of the bribe would be $50,000! Joe said that he would not pay this amount until he first met with the agent! The accountant then proposed that he and the agent split the $50,000. During this meeting, the accountant's wife also assisted in offering the bribe and became a defendant.

The agent did meet with Joe and they agreed to a lesser bribe. This meeting was recorded and brought the OC member directly into the investigation. Subsequently, the accountant paid the bribe, and I immediately arrested him. While searching his vehicle, I found a ledger book which recorded other bribes, and showed large amounts of cash flowing in and out of safe deposit boxes. This led to a $23 million bid rigging investigation, and the conviction of five additional OC members.

RECORDER I USED TO CAPTURE WORDS FOR TRIAL

The investigation of Joe and his accountant resulted in 20 hours of recorded conversation. Virtually every word of the 20 hours of conversation was captured on tape as evidence. That evidence - their words, could be replayed at any future trial. I painstakingly transcribed, as accurately as humanly possible, the 20 hours of conversation. After reviewing the transcripts, they were presented as evidence before a jury.

The jury heard the actual words and expressions exactly as they were spoken by the defendants, and by their own words they were found guilty and sentenced to jail. The heart of the government's case was that 20 hours of the defendants own words. The defense attorneys tried to attack both the undercover agent's character and mine, to confuse the jury. These attorneys tried other methods to make the defendants appear innocent as well. But the recorded words proved to be evidence the defense could not overcome. This resulted in their own words proving them guilty.

It is also interesting to note that although the defendants were tried for bribery, in a spiritual sense their own words convicted them of much more. Remember that only 20 hours out of a lifetime were recorded, yet they contained the use of the Lord's name in vain, general cursing, lies, talk of sexual immorality, greed, fraud, blackmail, extortion, and much more. If in only 20 hours all of these words were recorded, you can imagine what a lifetime of recording would disclose!

During another undercover investigation, the FBI used both audio and video to record several politicians taking bribes to help an Arab sheik. After the conviction of a congressman, jurors were reported to have said, "The tapes showed all," and "The real congressman was on the video tape and not on the witness stand."

If government agents can capture every word spoken during 20 hours of conversations, or produce video tapes for a portion of someone's lifetime which can convict them, imagine what a holy and righteous God can do with your lifetime!

The Bible speaks about God's judgment and your day before Him in court. It is called the Great White Throne Trial. The critical evidence will be your own words. Every word spoken over a person's entire lifetime will be used as evidence.

> Matthew 12:36,37 Every idle word that men speak they shall give account thereof on the day of judgment. For by your words you shall be justified and by your words you shall be condemned.

In addition to words, all actions, even those hidden or done in darkness, God will bring to light at that trial.

> Luke 12:2,3 For there is nothing covered, that shall not be revealed; neither hid, that shall not be known. Therefore whatsoever you have spoken in darkness shall be heard in the light; and that which you have spoken in the ear in closets shall be proclaimed upon the housetops.

You will be judged in perfect righteousness according to your own words, works, and thoughts. Yes, even your thoughts.

> Matthew 5:28 Whosoever looks upon a woman to lust after her has committed adultery already with her in his heart.

Who can stand before God and have his entire life reviewed? Who in his lifetime has never cursed, or lied, or stolen, or hated, or lusted, or had an impure thought? God is not interested in the number of sins you have committed because one is enough to separate you from Him.

The Bible says that all have sinned and fallen short of God's glory, that none are righteous, no not one, and that sin demands eternal separation from God. This is spiritual death. Without Jesus Christ, right now you are as a felon before God, deserving His wrath and judgment.

Hell: The Eternal Prison

The Bible reveals that God is holy, righteous and just. Because God is holy, He must punish sin. All sin results in the death penalty. This penalty means eternal separation from God in a place of torment called hell. Thus, hell can be viewed as a form of prison.

A person who breaks the penal code is called a felon, and is subject to the full punishment of the law. A person who breaks God's law is called a sinner. Thus, sin can be viewed as a felony against God's law. Under God's law there are no minor violations or misdemeanors, since every sin is a felony.

If you can understand that sin is as a felony to God, then you can easily understand God's legal system. You then will be able to understand why Jesus Christ had to die for your sins.

> 1 John 3:4 Whosoever committeth sin transgresseth also the law: for sin is the transgression of the law.

A person who sins is subject to the full penalty of the law, which is death:

> Romans 6:23 For the wages of sin is death...

On Judgment Day, all of a person's life will be examined and judged for sin. This judgment will include all actions, thoughts and words. Everything done during a lifetime will fall under God's judgment and nothing will escape Him. This will take place at what the Bible identifies as the Great White Throne Judgment or Trial.

> Revelation 20:11 And I saw a great white throne, and him that sat on it, from whose face the earth and the heaven fled away; and there was found no place for them.

31

(12) And I saw the dead, small and great, stand before God; and the books were opened: and another book was opened, which is the book of life: and the dead were judged out of those things which were written in the books, according to their works.

(13) And the sea gave up the dead which were in it; and death and hell delivered up the dead which were in them: *and they were judged every man according to their works.*

All of mankind, who have rejected Jesus Christ as Savior, will stand in judgment before Holy God. All sin will be accounted for and the sentence will be decreed by God. The sentence will be death. This separation from God is called the second death.

Revelation 20:14,15 And death and hell were cast into the lake of fire. This is **the second death**. And whosoever was not found written in the book of life was cast into the lake of fire.

Hell is not a joking matter. The death of Jesus Christ shows how seriously God takes the penalty of sin. Hell is the place where sinners/felons go for breaking God's law, just as prison is the place where criminals go for breaking man's law. If you understand man's legal system, then it is easy to understand God's legal system. The difference is that, God's judgment is perfect.

God's judgment is the same for everyone, with no exceptions. Everyone's life is judged according to God's penal code, which is found in the Bible. All have committed sin before God. If you leave this life without Jesus Christ as your Lord and Savior, you will be eternally separated from God in His prison, which is hell.

CHAPTER TWO

JESUS CHRIST FACED THE LEGAL SYSTEM

A simple study of the Bible shows that Jesus Christ went through the entire legal process of His day. This system closely resembled our legal system. Remember when you read this section, that Jesus Christ was innocent of all the charges against Him. He allowed Himself to be treated as a criminal for the redemption of mankind.

The Lord never, on any occasion, sinned. He broke neither man's nor God's law. He is the sinless, only begotten Son of God. Again, when reading this section, remember He was sinless and innocent of any crime.

- **Arrested: John 18:3,12**

Jesus Christ healed the sick, fed the multitudes and spoke truth, and yet a large number of soldiers came to arrest Him. He then was brought before the authorities to face a mock trial. Do you think He was advised of His Constitutional rights?

The Lord knows what it is like to be publicly arrested and bound (handcuffed) by the police.

"Judas then, having received a band of men and officers from the chief priests and Pharisees, cometh thither with lanterns and torches and weapons...Then the band and the captain and officers of the Jews took Jesus, and **bound** him."

• **Close Friend Informed; He Was Set Up:** **Matthew 26:14-16**

Judas was one of Jesus' most trusted disciples. He held all of the money and gave it out as needed. One of the Lord's closest and most trusted friends set Him up for money. Judas was given 30 pieces of silver for betraying the Son of God! He told the authorities where Jesus stayed at night, so that they knew where to find Him for the arrest.

Even though you may be guilty of the crime, was someone an informer in your case? The Lord knows all about it.

"Then one of the twelve, called Judas Iscariot, went unto the chief priests, And said unto them, What will ye give me, and I will deliver him unto you? And they covenanted with him for thirty pieces of silver. And from that time he sought opportunity to **betray him**."

• **After His Arrest, All of His Friends Left Him: Mark 14:50**

The Lord spent years with His disciples, but at His arrest they all fled from Him. He was deserted and faced the authorities by Himself. He was not given a legal-aid attorney. He faced the trial alone. One disciple even denied Him when He was confronted with being an associate of Jesus.

When you were arrested, did all of your friends leave you? The Lord knows all about it.

"And they all **forsook him**, and fled."

- **Interrogated; Questioned By The Authorities: Luke 22:66-71**

The leading authorities of the day questioned Him. Jesus' crime was that He claimed to be the Christ, the Son of God which they viewed as the crime of blasphemy. Were you questioned by the police and other government authorities?

The Lord knows all about it.

> "The **elders of the people** and the **chief priests** and the **scribes** came together, and led him into their council, **saying**, Art thou the Christ? tell us. And he said unto them, If I tell you, ye will not believe: And if I also ask you, ye will not answer me, nor let me go...then said they all, Art thou then the Son of God? And he said unto them, Ye say that I am...And they said, What need we any further witness? for we ourselves have heard of his own mouth."

- **False Witnesses: Matthew 26:59,60**

Jesus Christ never committed one crime during His entire life; therefore, many false witnesses came forth to try and frame Him. They gave false testimony so that charges could be brought against Him, but they could not agree on their lies.

Did a false witness testify against you? Jesus Christ knows all about it.

> "Now the chief priests, and elders, and all the council, sought **false witness** against Jesus, to put him to death; But found none: yea, though many false witnesses came, yet found they none. At the last came **two false witnesses.**"

- **Indicted: Matthew 26: 65,66**

Jesus Christ stood before the grand jury of His day and was indicted. The charge was blasphemy in that He claimed to be the Son of God, the Savior of mankind. Conviction for this crime meant the death penalty.

The authorities refused proof that He was the Son of God. The healings and many miracles He performed, along with the feeding of the multitudes, did not matter. Jesus Christ even raised people from the dead, in sight of large crowds, but nothing mattered to the authorities. He was interfering with the religious system of the day, and its leaders wanted Him out of the way.

Were you indicted or do you have to face the grand jury? The Lord Jesus knows all about it.

> "Then the high priest rent his clothes, saying, He hath spoken blasphemy; what further need have we of witnesses? behold, now ye have heard his blasphemy. What think ye? **They answered and said, He is guilty of death.**"

- **Indictment Charge: John 19:7**

The charge against Jesus Christ was blasphemy because He claimed to be the Son of God. The authorities all were aware of His miracles which proved He was the Savior. This charge carried the death sentence. Jesus never answered His accusers. He was silent before them, as they charged Him with this crime. He knew that the trial was rigged against Him.

How did it feel to have the indictment read to you? Jesus Christ knows exactly what it is like.

> "The Jews answered him, We have a law, **and by our law he ought to die, because he made himself the Son of God**."

- **Cruel Guards Beat Him: Matthew 26:67 and Matthew 27:30**

The Bible says that Jesus Christ was beaten so severely that He was unrecognizable. He was beaten with rods on the face, and His beard was pulled out. His back was beaten with a whip, which is called flogging. A crown with huge thorns was placed on His head and driven into His skull! The pain of this torture had to be incredible.

This is what Jesus Christ endured before He went to the cross and died for the sin of mankind. This was all part of the price He paid for our sin, so that we do not have to pay ourselves.

There is nothing that a cruel guard can do to you that was not done already to the Lord. He did real, "hard time."

> "Then did they spit in his face, and **buffeted him**; and others smote him with the palms

of their hands, And they spit upon him, and took the reed, **and smote him** on the head."

- **Trial: Matthew 27:2,11**

Jesus Christ stood trial before the Roman government. He faced the death penalty as an innocent man. All proof in His favor was ignored because they wanted Him out of the way. This was necessary to condemn Him, so He could shed His blood on the cross and pay the penalty for sin.

Even though you are guilty of a crime, the Lord Jesus knows what you went through.

> "And when they had bound him, they led him away, **and delivered him to Pontius Pilate** the governor. And Jesus stood before the governor: and the governor asked him, saying, Art thou the King of the Jews? And Jesus said unto him, Thou sayest."

- **His Case Was Appealed: Luke 23:7,11**

> "And as soon as he (Pontius Pilate) knew that he belonged unto Herod's jurisdiction, he sent him to Herod, who himself also was at Jerusalem at that time....Then he questioned with him in many words; but he answered him nothing....And the chief priests and scribes stood and vehemently accused him....And Herod with his men of war set him at nought, and mocked him, and arrayed him in a gorgeous robe, and sent him again to Pilate."

- ## Lost Trial and Public Execution: Matthew 27:31,39,41

The Lord was found guilty and sentenced to death by crucifixion. This is one of the most horrible ways to die ever imagined. Huge nails are driven into the person's hands and feet, then he is nailed to the cross. This is exactly what was done to Jesus Christ.

His cross was placed upright with all of the body weight pulling down on the nails. He had to pull up to breathe. It was a terrible, slow death in horrible pain. Remember, Jesus Christ was the Son of God and innocent of all the charges.

If you face a long time in jail, or even the death penalty, Jesus Christ knows exactly what it is like. He has been there!

> "And led him away to crucify him.... And they that passed by reviled him, wagging their heads,...Likewise also the chief priests mocking him, with the scribes and elders,"

- ## Given Terrible Fluids to Drink: Matthew 27:34

During His execution, Jesus Christ was given sour wine mixed with gall. Gall is like slime from bile and has a very nasty taste. He refused to take it.

Christ knows what prison life is really like.

> "They gave him vinegar **to drink** mingled with gall: and when he had tasted thereof, he would not drink."

- ## Jesus Christ Was Rejected and Lonely: Matthew 27:46

When Christ was arrested, all His disciples fled from Him. He faced the authorities by Himself. There was no one to help Him. At His trial, He faced an angry crowd who yelled, *"Crucify Him, Crucify Him."* While He was hanging on the cross, the crowd mocked Him. Only His mother and a few women stayed with Him as He died. God the Father even turned away from Jesus while He was on the cross. The Father turned away, because on the cross Jesus Christ became sin!

> 1Peter 2:24 Who his own self bare our sins in his own body on the tree, that we, being dead to sins, should live unto righteousness: by whose stripes ye were healed.

Are you lonely in prison? Who is not? No one can be any lonelier than Jesus Christ was on that cross. He died separated from both God and man. Probably the very last people He spoke with were the two dying criminals, who were next to Him.

Jesus Christ knows what it is to be rejected.

> "And about the ninth hour Jesus cried with a loud voice, saying, Eli, Eli, lama sabachthani? that is to say, My God, my God, **why hast thou forsaken me**?"

- **Jesus Died In The Place of a Criminal: Matthew 27:15-17, 20,26**

At the time of Jesus, there was a custom during the feast of Passover, of setting one criminal free. A criminal named Barabbas was condemned to death and offered freedom, and Pontius Pilate, the Roman judge, offered to let Jesus go in place of him. This failed, as the people wanted Jesus killed. So Barabbas was freed, and the innocent Jesus Christ died in his place.

This is a picture of the Lord Jesus dying in the place of sinners - including those in prison!

> "Now **at that feast the governor was wont to release unto the people a prisoner**, whom they would. And they had then a notable prisoner, called Barabbas. Therefore when they were gathered together, Pilate said unto them, Whom will ye that I release unto you? Barabbas, or Jesus which is called Christ?... But the chief priests and elders persuaded the multitude that they should ask Barabbas, and destroy Jesus... **Then released he Barabbas** unto them: and when he had scourged Jesus, he delivered him to be crucified."

- **He Died Between Two Criminals: Luke 23:32,33**

The Lord Jesus was the sinless, only begotten Son of God and yet was executed in the same location where all criminals were crucified. When Christ was crucified, two criminals were killed with Him. He died between them. The Son of God died as a common criminal, and with criminals.

The Lord Jesus knows what it is to feel like a criminal because that is how He died.

> "And there were also two other, malefactors (criminals), led with him to be put to death. And when they were come to the place, which is called Calvary, there they crucified him, and the malefactors, one on the right hand, and the other on the left."

CHAPTER THREE

JESUS CHRIST YOUR ADVOCATE/DEFENSE ATTORNEY

Advocate: *One that pleads the cause of another, specifically, one that pleads the cause of another before a tribunal or judicial court*

When a person is arrested and faces serious criminal charges, he wants the best defense attorney possible to represent him. If the charge could result in the death penalty, he would sell all of his possessions to obtain the best attorney. With God, the penalty for committing sin is death; therefore, before God's court of law, a person wants the very best attorney to represent him. The stakes are too high for anything less than the best.

God in His love provided this attorney for you. He provided an Attorney who was willing to take your sin and die in your place! He provided Jesus Christ to defend you. The word used in the Bible for attorney is advocate. Jesus Christ comes along side of you to plead your case.

In God's legal system, the Lord Jesus is there to plead the case for all those who want Him to be their Advocate.

Christ turns no one away who comes to Him. There is no charge for Christ to be an Advocate, since He only responds to someone's faith.

> 1 John 2:1 My little children, these things write I unto you, that ye sin not. And if any man sin, we have an **advocate** (Attorney) with the Father, Jesus Christ the righteous:

UNITED STATES SUPREME COURT

With Jesus Christ defending you, how you can lose? Christ already has paid the price for your sin. With the Lord as your Attorney, you have all of your sins forgiven and assurance of eternal life with God. Jesus has paid the price for your sins, and He now intercedes for you before God the Father. The shed blood of Jesus Christ, God's chosen Advocate, guarantees your freedom from the eternal death penalty in hell. Jesus always is interceding on your behalf.

Romans 8:34 Who is he that condemneth?
It is Christ that died, yea rather, that is risen
again, who is even at the right hand of God,
who also maketh intercession for us.

Because the Lord Jesus is your defense attorney, you
can have absolute assurance of eternal life. You can have
assurance that all of your sins are forgiven and you can
be at peace with God. With Christ as your Advocate, how
can you ever lose? What is required on your part is to
repent for your life of sin, and then to call on Christ for forgiveness of sin and receive Him as your Lord and Savior.
With Jesus Christ as your Savior, based on the word of
God, you have assurance of eternal life.

Hebrews 7:25 Wherefore he is able also to
save them to the uttermost that come unto
God by him, seeing he ever liveth to make
intercession for them.

Jesus Christ Died on the Cross
Accused as a Criminal

Luke 23:32 And there were also two other,
malefactors [criminals], led with him to be
put to death.

It may be difficult to see the connection between the
death of Jesus Christ on the cross nearly 2,000 years
ago and your life today. Perhaps you cannot see how His
death could have any effect on you today, when you are
in prison and behind bars.

47

Although Jesus Christ is honored and worshipped today by millions, 2,000 years ago He was arrested as a **criminal**; tried as a **criminal**; and executed as a **criminal**! He died in the place of a **criminal** and hung on the cross between two condemned **criminals**. Jesus Christ died by crucifixion because this was the way criminals were executed under Roman law.

Because Jesus Christ went through the entire process as a **criminal**, He knows exactly what you are going through. The Lord can help you in prison. He knows exactly what it is like.

The Bible reveals that Jesus Christ was not just an ordinary man. He was God in a human body. This is an awesome thought, that God became a man and walked amongst us!

> 2 Corinthians 5:19 To wit, that God was in Christ, reconciling the world unto himself ...

God loves you so much that He became a man, so that He could know personally what you are going through in life and aid you:

> Hebrews 2:17,18 Wherefore in all things it behoved him to be made like unto his brethren, that he might be a merciful and faithful high priest...(18) For in that he himself hath suffered being tempted, he is able to succour (aid, help) them that are tempted.

God is not far away and unconcerned about you, but He loves you and sent Jesus so you can have eternal life with Him. God personally cares for you and loves you. Maybe you have no one in the world who loves you, but that does not change God's love for you. The sure proof of God's love for you is that He sent Jesus Christ into the world, so that you might not perish in eternity but have eternal life with God.

There are no tests which you face in this life that Jesus Christ has not already faced and overcome. The Lord Jesus faced every procedure in the legal system, including the death penalty. Christ knows exactly what you are going through, and even though you are guilty of breaking the law, the Lord wants to forgive you for all of your sins and face the problems with you.

> Hebrews 4:15 For we have not an high priest which cannot be touched with the feeling of our infirmities; but was in all points tempted like as we are, yet without sin.

You might be in prison without a friend in the world. Maybe your family has left you. Maybe you are severely depressed because your life has been ruined or you face a long prison sentence. Maybe you are thinking of suicide. Because the Lord Jesus went through the entire legal system, God personally knows what you are going through. He wants to forgive you for all of your sins and to go through prison with you.

God wants to put peace and joy in your life, even though you may be in prison. With Christ walking with you, you can have peace and joy, even in prison, and there is no reason to fear.

> John 14:27 Peace I leave with you, my peace I give unto you: not as the world giveth, give I unto you. Let not your heart be troubled, neither let it be afraid.

The Lord Jesus never failed. Everything the world threw at Him, He overcame. He never sinned, not once. Jesus Christ wants to break the hold that fear, depression, hate, violence, alcohol, and immoral sex may have over you, and replace this hold with His love, peace, joy, and power. Because the Lord never sinned and overcame the world, when you trust Him as your Lord and Savior, you too can have God's peace in your life.

The amazing thing about Jesus Christ and your life in prison is that there is nothing, I repeat, there is nothing in prison which you face that He has not faced already. The Lord Jesus was not afraid to be treated as a criminal. This was needed so that He could pay the price for sin, and thus, you can have eternal life with God now.

Right now, even if you are on death row, Jesus Christ can give you inner peace and go through it with you. Remember, He already was executed as a criminal, and because He rose from the dead, He can help you personally.

Christ Took The "Rap" For You

While it is true that God is holy, righteous, just, and that He must punish sinners, God really loves man and sent Jesus Christ as the Savior for mankind. God loves you so much that He was willing to become a man and die a horrible death so you would not have to face eternity separated from Him in God's prison. On the cross Jesus Christ took all of the punishment that you deserved for breaking God's law.

> Isaiah 53:5 But he was wounded for our transgressions, he was bruised for our iniquities: the chastisement of our peace was upon him; and with his stripes we are

healed. (6) All we like sheep have gone astray; we have turned every one to his own way; and the LORD hath laid on him the iniquity of us all.

Although He was sinless, He died as a sinner separated from God the Father. On the cross, He shouted out, *"My God, my God, why hast thou forsaken me?"* as He bore our sin. God the Father turned His back to the Son.

The reason God the Father turned from Jesus on the cross was because Christ became sin as He was paying the penalty for sin. He paid the full penalty for sin with His death. He paid the price for sin, so those who believe in Him could be free from the death sentence. Jesus Christ died in your place:

Hebrews 2:9 He should taste death for every man.

In modern terms, Jesus Christ took the full "rap" for your sin. As your Attorney, He became a "felon" for you and took the full penalty of God's law. The sinless Son of God became sin, so you could have forgiveness and assurance of eternal life with God. With Him as your Advocate, the trial is "rigged" in your favor!

God made a trade with mankind. Through the death of the Lord Jesus, He takes our sin, and then replaces it with Christ's righteousness. To be righteous means to be able to stand before God without sin. The verses to show this follow:

2 Corinthians 5:21 For he hath made him **to be sin for us**, who knew no sin, that we might be made the righteousness of God in him.

1 Peter 3:18 For Christ also hath once suffered for sins, **the just for the unjust**, that he might bring us to God, being put to death in the flesh, but quickened by the Spirit

The death of Jesus Christ nearly 2,000 years ago is very important to you today. By having faith that Jesus Christ died on the cross for your sin, you can be set free from the penalty for sin. God loves everyone equally. He loves you in prison just as much as He loves a person who is walking free in the street. Through faith in the Lord Jesus and what He did on the cross, you can be forgiven of all your sins! Yes, all of them.

Colossians 1:14 In whom we have redemption through his blood, even the forgiveness of sins

You do not have to, "clean-up your act" to come to Christ. God loves you just as you are right now. When you come to Jesus in repentance for your sins, He will "clean-up your act." Even if you were a Barabbas, a murderer, through faith in Jesus Christ you can be forgiven of sin and be at peace with God and with yourself.

> Romans 5:8 But God commendeth his love toward us, in that, while we were yet sinners, Christ died for us.

EVEN U.S. SUPREME COURT JUSTICES ARE SUBJECT TO GOD'S DIVINE COURT

CHAPTER FOUR

GOD CAN FORGIVE AND SAVE ANYONE

Tamar, Rahab, Ruth and Bathsheba

The Bible reveals the supernatural birth of Jesus. His mother was a virgin; therefore, He was born without the sin nature of mankind. The Bible also gives the genealogy of Jesus Christ's stepfather. This is the family He would be raised in and with which he would be identified. Jesus' stepfather was a descendant of a long line of royalty, the kings of Israel. His genealogy can be traced through Abraham and King David.

When you study His genealogy in Matthew, Chapter 1, something unusual is revealed. The genealogy lists all men, with the exception of four women. These women are Tamar, Rahab the harlot, Ruth the Moabitess, and Bathsheba.

The amazing thing about the Lord's adopted genealogy is the background of each woman. Tamar used deception to talk her father-in-law into having sexual relations with her. Rahab was a pagan harlot. Ruth was a pagan and a social outcast, while Bathsheba was involved in adultery with King David. David and Bathsheba had a son named

Solomon who became king after David. He also is in the Lord's genealogy.

The Bible does not hide these women but actually lists them for all to see in the Lord's genealogy. Most people would try and hide such things, but Jesus was not ashamed of them. There was a reason He was not ashamed of them.

The Bible says that Rahab was a harlot who lived in the pagan city of Jericho. She proved her love for God by helping the Jews as they entered into the Promised Land. When the city was destroyed, she and her family were the only ones spared. She married a Jewish man and became part of the direct line of the Lord Jesus.

Think of this, a pagan harlot was a direct ancestor of the Son of God! When she turned from her sin to the living God, He forgave her for all of the paganism. She then was listed in the Lord's adopted genealogy for everyone to see.

Ruth was from the nation of Moab. Moab was a pagan country, and they practiced sinful rites which were forbidden by God. These rites included burning their children alive as sacrifices. Because they were pagans, the Moabites were outcasts and rejected by the Jews. Although Ruth came from this background, she turned from it. She repented of the paganism, and like Rahab, she turned to the living God. Ruth was accepted and married a Jewish man named Boaz. She became the grandmother of King David. Her story even became one of the books of the Bible, the Book of Ruth.

Rahab and Ruth are both examples of how completely God forgives sin. No matter what their background of sin, God forgave them.

Both of these pagan women were so completely forgiven by God that He allowed them to become direct descendants of the Lord Jesus. If God completely forgave and accepted Rahab and Ruth, He also will forgive and accept you completely. Even if your background is as bad as Rahab's, you can be completely forgiven and accepted, just as she was. Even if you are a social outcast and rejected like Ruth was, God will completely accept you.

God does not care about where you were born, the color of your skin, how much wealth you have, or your social position. Ruth and Rahab are perfect examples that anyone can be completely forgiven and accepted by God. It does not matter whether you are a male or a female.

The Tale of the Two Thieves: Which One are You?

The Lord Jesus died between two thieves. One thief rejected Christ and challenged Jesus to come down from the cross and save them. The second criminal recognized that he was a sinner. He feared God because of his sin. He realized that Jesus was sinless and had done nothing wrong. He called Jesus, "**Lord.**" This dying thief then said something amazing; he said, *"Remember me when thou comest into thy kingdom."* That dying thief knew Jesus was dying for his sin, and Jesus would be glorified in His kingdom!

Again, you now have the same choice that these two criminals had. Are you going to be like the thief who rejected Christ and went into hell, to be eternally separated from God? Or, are you going to repent of your sin and call Jesus, "Lord" saying, *"Remember me when you comest into thy kingdom."* You now have the same choice that these two criminals had.

One dying thief simply admitted he was a sinner and he called Jesus, "Lord." That thief did not "clean-up" his life, or join a church, or do good works for salvation. He simply repented of his sin, called Jesus, "Lord," and recognized that Jesus was the Savior.

Just as the dying thief received forgiveness of his sin and eternal life, so right now you also can have the assurance of eternal life with God. The Lord Jesus loves you just as much as He loved that dying thief 2,000 years ago. Come to Jesus now. Repent of your sin, and confess Christ as your Lord and Savior.

Jesus Christ loves you and died on the cross for you. He wants to be your Advocate before God's court of law. Are you going to try to defend yourself before God in His court of law, or are you going to have Jesus of Nazareth as your Advocate?

God does not ask any more of you than does the United States' court system. But in God's system, you have the right to a court appointed attorney, who will go to jail in your place; however, in either system, if you refuse an attorney, then you will have to stand alone against the full power of the government. This includes facing the death penalty for breaking the law!

The Tale of Two Dying Criminals

Luke 23:32 "And there were also two other, malefactors [criminals, thieves] led with him to be put to death.

(33) And when they were come to the place, which is called Calvary, there they crucified him, and the malefactors, one on the right hand, and the other on the left.

(34) Then said Jesus, Father, forgive them; for they know not what they do. And they parted his raiment, and cast lots.

(39) And one of the malefactors which were hanged railed on him, saying, If thou be Christ, save thyself and us.

(40) But the other answering rebuked him, saying, **Dost not thou fear God**, seeing thou art in the same condemnation?

(41) And we indeed justly; for we receive the due reward of our deeds: but this man hath done nothing amiss.

(42) And he said unto Jesus, **Lord**, remember me when thou comest into thy kingdom.

(43) And Jesus said unto him, Verily I say unto thee, **Today shalt thou be with me in paradise."**

The End Story of the Accountant and his Wife

Previously I had mentioned the Organized Crime accountant and his wife who were convicted of bribery. The accountant was sentenced to prison but his wife was not. When the accountant was arrested, he was in possession of a ledger book, which contained a record of a large amount of funds going in and out of several safe deposit boxes. It turns out that these safe deposit boxes were used to store money that was part of a $23 million bid rigging scheme.

The accountant was brought before a grand jury to testify about the ledger book. He lied and hid the truth about the funds. OC members had promised that if he refused to cooperate with the government and lied to the grand jury about the ledger book, they would provide for his wife while he was in prison. They also promised to pay his legal expenses, and provide him with employment after he was released from prison.

The OC members failed to keep any of their promises, which resulted in great suffering for his wife. He also was traumatized by his stay in prison, and was fearful that he would be convicted and imprisoned for perjury because of his grand jury testimony. When he was released from prison, immediately he went to the United States Attorney to cooperate about the ledger book. His cooperation resulted in the conviction of five OC figures.

Because I initially had seized the ledger book, I was called as a witness. While preparing to testify, I met the accountant's wife. She came right up to me and said, "I have no hard feelings against you." I told her, "The investigation was just business." She went on to share that life became unbearable after her husband had gone to prison because she was starving, had lost her house, and was forced to live with friends and relatives. She then said that the entire experience had led her to repent of sin and to trust in Jesus Christ as her Savior.

I shared my faith in Jesus Christ with her, and she became very excited. She told me going through all of that turmoil had been necessary for her to trust in Christ as her Savior, but it was worth it. In her excited state she said that her husband also had come to believe in Jesus Christ, and she wanted me to meet with him. I followed her into a room, and in a loud and excited voice she called to her husband and said, "Agent McTernan believes in Jesus like we do!" I shook hands with him and we briefly spoke about Jesus. I then was called out of the room to prepare my testimony.

What a wonderful example this is of God's forgiveness. A man who was deeply involved with Organized Crime was forgiven by God, and now both he and his wife could live a life of peace with Jesus Christ as their Savior. God turns no one away who repents of sin and trusts in Jesus Christ as Savior.

> Matthew 11:28 Come unto me, all ye that labour and are heavy laden, and I will give you rest.

CHAPTER FIVE

TURN TO THE LORD

God Can Use You in Prison

J ust because you are in prison, that does not mean God cannot work with you and use you. The Bible gives several examples of how God used people in prison. If you are willing to study the Bible, and to trust and obey His word, God can use you wherever you are. Let's look in the Bible at some examples of how God used people in prison.

- Joseph, the son of Jacob

At a very young age, Joseph was called to be a leader of the Jewish people. Because of this calling, his brothers were jealous of him and sold him into slavery. He was taken to Egypt where he lived a godly life as a slave, yet he was falsely accused of a crime and thrown into prison for more than 10 years. While in prison, Joseph found favor with the guards, and they actually trusted him enough to place him into a position of authority.

Genesis 39:21,22 But the LORD was with Joseph, and showed him mercy, and gave him favour in the sight of the keeper of **the prison**. And the keeper of **the prison** committed to Joseph's hand all the prisoners that were in **the prison**; and whatsoever they did there, he was the doer of it.

Although Joseph was unjustly cast into prison for a crime he did not commit, his trust in God never wavered. The Bible says that God was allowing Joseph to be tested and tried as preparation for a tremendous task, thus prison was a training ground.

After all of those years in prison, Joseph came to the attention of Pharaoh, the king of Egypt. Pharaoh took Joseph out of prison and made him second in charge of the entire kingdom. God gave Joseph knowledge and wisdom to save the people from a severe drought that was coming. His brothers, who had sold him into slavery, also were saved.

The Bible says that Joseph's stay in prison was not wasted but rather, it was a time of testing, so that he could be trusted with the authority over Pharaoh's entire kingdom.

> Psalm 105:17-21 He sent a man before them, even Joseph, who was sold for a servant: Whose feet they hurt with fetters: he was laid in iron: Until the time that his word came: the word of the LORD tried him. The king sent and loosed him; even the ruler of the people, and let him go free. He made him lord of his house, and ruler of all his substance:

- The Apostle Paul

The Apostle Paul was placed in prison for preaching the gospel. He had committed no crime. While in jail, Paul wrote many of the New Testament books of the Bible. God was able to use Paul even while he was locked in a terrible Roman prison. He knew that the word of God could not be stopped. This is what Paul said about being bound:

> 2 Timothy 2:9 Wherein I suffer trouble, as an evil doer, even unto bonds; but the word of God is not bound.

- The Apostle John

The book of Revelation, the last book of the Bible was written by John. This book, which so clearly shows the defeat of evil and the glorious Second Coming of Jesus Christ, was written while John was exiled and isolated on an island. This happened because he was preaching the gospel, just as the Apostle Paul had been.

Although John was confined, God still spoke to him and used him to write the Book of Revelation. Being imprisoned stopped neither Paul nor John, and it cannot stop you.

> Revelation 1:9 I John, who also am your brother, and companion in tribulation, and in the kingdom and patience of Jesus Christ, was in the isle that is called Patmos, for the word of God, and for the testimony of Jesus Christ.

If you trust God, He can use you in prison. The word of God is not bound, and as God used Joseph's time in prison to train him to be one of the most powerful men of his day, your time in prison does not have to be wasted. You can learn of God and His ways in prison as Joseph did. It is even possible that you could be used by God in an awesome way as He used Joseph. God can work with you right where you are.

If You Confess With Your Mouth

The Creator of the universe knows exactly what it is like to be in prison. He was there through Jesus Christ. God can comfort you like a loving Father. The Lord is not some far-off, mystical being to whom you cannot relate. God will go all the way with you in prison - even if it is through the death penalty, *I will never leave thee, nor forsake thee.* Jesus Christ walked your road 2,000 years ago. He desires to be your Advocate.

Remember Matthew 12:37 *For by your words you shall be justified and by your words you shall be condemned.* Right now by your own words, spoken from your heart, you can be justified before God. No depth of sin is too great for Him to forgive.

The Bible says that right now you can escape the Great White Throne Judgment. You can escape the humiliation of having all of your sins brought to light. You can escape the horror of standing in your sin before a Holy God.

You can escape judgment by receiving the Lord Jesus into your life as your Savior. He already has taken the full penalty for all of your sins; His blood was shed and the wrath of God's law was served on Christ. God is now free to give you a divine pardon, and to release you into a new life because of the Lord Jesus Christ's finished work on the cross.

God promises that all who are in Christ are new creations; old things pass away and the same power that raised the Lord from the dead will raise you also. Christ's power working in you now will keep you from living a life of sin.

If you believe that the thoughts, words and actions of your lifetime condemn you before God, now is the time that your own words can justify you. If you now confess Jesus Christ as your Lord and Savior/Advocate, you will be forgiven.

IF YOU CONFESS WITH YOUR MOUTH

Romans 10:9 "That if you confess with your mouth the Lord Jesus, and shall believe in your heart that God raised him from the dead, you shall be saved."

This confession involves truly repenting for your past life of sin, and changing your focus to live with Jesus Christ as the center of your life. You can have complete forgiveness for your sin and the power of God in your life right now, by coming to God in prayer and confessing Jesus Christ as your Lord and Savior. A prayer like this will do:

God, I realize Your Son, Jesus Christ, shed His blood on the cross and died for me. I realize that only through faith in Jesus Christ can I escape the penalty for sin, which is hell. I now repent and turn away from my self-centered life of sin, and confess Jesus Christ as my Lord and Savior. I realize you have completely forgiven me for all of my sins. I know that I now have eternal life because Jesus died for me, and He now is my Lord and Savior. Through faith in the Lord Jesus, I am now a new creation, and sin no longer has power over me. Thank you for sending your Son to die for me.

Romans 10:13 For whosoever calls upon the name of the Lord shall be saved.

CHAPTER SIX

OPENING THE PRISON TO THEM THAT ARE BOUND

Isaiah 61:1 The Spirit of the Lord GOD … hath sent me to bind up the brokenhearted, to proclaim liberty to the captives, **and the opening of the prison to them that are bound;**

God's Rehabilitation: A New Heart

The Bible reveals what causes man to commit sin. Sometimes this sin involves breaking the law and the person ends up in prison. What man calls a crime, God calls sin. The problem with sin is that its roots lie within the heart of man. Jeremiah the prophet said,

The heart is deceitful above all things, and desperately wicked: who can know it?

Man's nature is deceitful and wicked, and this is the source of sin. The Lord Jesus pinpointed the root of crime and sin. Like Jeremiah, He also said it was within the heart of man.

> Mark 7:21-23 For from within, out of the heart of men, proceed evil thoughts, adulteries, fornications, murders, thefts, covetousness, wickedness, deceit, lasciviousness, an evil eye, blasphemy, pride, foolishness: All these evil things come from within, and defile the man.

The Bible clearly shows that the heart of man is the source of evil. Sometimes the evil is subtle and involves sins like hatred and lying. These sins do not break mans' criminal law, but they are still evil. While bank robbery and murder are more obvious types of evil, all evil comes from the same source, the heart of man.

Today, literally billions of dollars have been spent by the government to try and rehabilitate criminals. Every technique of psychology and every form of education have been tried with very little success. These programs last a few years and then are discarded. The reason these programs do not work is that they fail to touch man's heart, where the sin nature lies. These programs can reach the mind, but not the heart. Man needs to have a "heart transplant" to be freed from this evil nature.

God says that if you will trust Jesus as your Savior, He will take your heart of stone (the sin nature) out and replace it with a new heart.. How many times have you tried to stop sinning only to fall right back into it? The pull of the old heart is always back toward sin. The real rehabilitation happens when God replaces the evil, broken heart with a new one.

Only God can put a new heart in you. The government cannot do it. You cannot do it by yourself. God does not patch up the old heart, but instead He gives you a brand new one! Only through Jesus Christ can God can give you a new heart.

Ezekiel 36:26 A new heart also will I give you, and a new spirit will I put within you: and I will take away the stony heart out of your flesh, and I will give you an heart of flesh.

A Prison Without Bars

You do not have to live behind bars to be in prison. Prison is a place where you are kept against your will. In prison, you are restrained; you are not free to go when you want, and where you want. The walls and fences of a prison are obstacles which restrain your freedom and will.

The Bible shows that you can be free on the outside but imprisoned by sin on the inside. Sin in the heart acts like handcuffs and chains on the soul. It shackles you to its power. The power of sin keeps you locked in confinement in the same way that those high walls and fences do.

The power of sin is real, not a myth. How many are imprisoned by drugs and cannot get free? How many are imprisoned by alcohol and are literal slaves to the bottle? How many are imprisoned by hatred and violence? The list of sins which can imprison a person are endless. The power of sin is like an awesome barbed-wire fence that you cannot get over. It's a terrible thing to be imprisoned by sin with no hope of freedom.

The Bible shows that you can know to do what is good and right, yet find that you cannot do it because the power of sin has you in its prison. You can want to do what is right, but something blocks you from doing it. The Bible calls this inner prison, "the law of sin and death." There is no escaping from this prison on your own. You do not have to be in a physical jail to be imprisoned. Even though you may be free from mans' jail, you still can be imprisoned to "the law of sin and death." Without Jesus Christ this is a lifetime sentence!

The Scriptures show how the prison of sin works. The law of sin is part of us, and it operates in our being. It is a force that only God, through the power of His Holy Spirit, can break. It has taken us captive and we are shackled to its power.

Romans 7:19 For the good that I would I do not: but the evil which I would not, that I do. (20) Now if I do that I would not, it is no more I that do it, but **sin that dwelleth in me.**

(23) But I see **another law in my members**, warring against the law of my mind, and bringing me into captivity to **the law of sin** which is in my members."

God sent Jesus to rip open the handcuffs of sin and to set you free from the bondage of its high prison walls. Jesus came to empower your life and to free you from a terrible prison. He frees you from the chains of the bottle or the needle, and from the prison of hatred and violence.

> Romans 8:2 For the law of the Spirit of life
> in Christ Jesus hath made me free from the
> law of sin and death.

Look at what the Lord Jesus has done for you. He took the penalty for your sin and then He became your court-appointed Defense Attorney. But this is not all Jesus did because as a warden, He sets you free from the high walls and handcuffs created by the law of sin and death. The Lord has the authority and power to free you from both the penalty and the prison of sin. There is no social program or drug that can do this. He alone has this authority.

The Healing of the Broken Heart

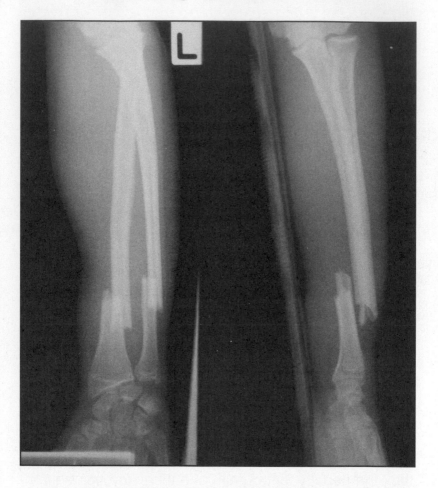

The Bible uses graphic words to describe what happens when a heart is broken. The picture is one of violent tearing and fracturing that shatters an object into pieces. If you ever have seen a picture of a severely fractured bone, this is what a broken heart looks like spiritually! A fractured bone needs an operation to put all of the pieces back together, and so it is with a fractured heart.

Within the broken heart lies anger, fear, anxiety, terror, trauma, hatred, and bitterness, and these emotions are what lead to panic attacks, depression, and the need for drugs or alcohol. It is the broken heart that generates these emotions but they are only symptoms. The real problem is a broken and fractured heart.

There are many things that can break a heart and it seems especially easy to break the heart of a child. The following is a list of things that can break a heart:

Divorce (This is especially devastating to children.)
Child Abuse (This includes physical, mental or
sexual abuse.)
Abortion (This is incredibly devastating to a woman and
needs special attention.)
Rejection (This is at the root of most broken hearts.)
Hatred (The Bible warns about provoking children
to wrath.)
Abandonment
War
Tragedy
Death

Because of the curse of sin, this world is designed to break the heart. Once the heart is broken, there is nothing on earth that can fix it. Psychology, with all of its drugs, cannot heal it. There are self-help programs with various steps to peace, but they cannot heal it, nor can religion. The effects of the broken heart only can be lessened or managed by these methods.

There is nothing on earth that can heal a broken heart because the root problem is spiritual. Jesus

Christ is the only one who can heal a broken heart. One of His titles is "The Great Physician," whom God sent to heal the brokenhearted.

>   Matthew 9:12 But when Jesus heard that, he said unto them, They that be whole need not a physician, but they that are sick.

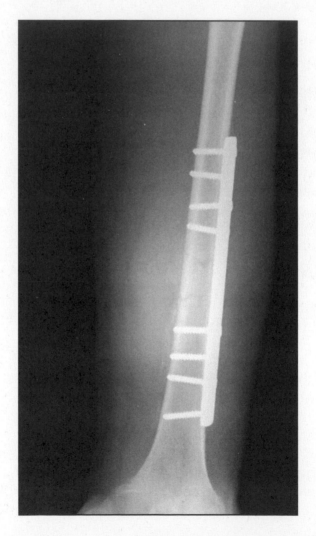

If a leg was severely fractured, a doctor would put all of the bones back into place and bind the break. This might involve putting screws in the bone and then putting a cast around it. This is exactly the way the Great Physician heals the broken heart. He takes all of the broken pieces and puts them together, then binds up the heart so that it can heal and remain healed!

The Bible also calls a broken heart a "heart of stone," but the heart healed by Jesus Christ is called a "heart of flesh." Stone is hard and cold, while flesh is alive to God. The work of God in your heart can be viewed as a spiritual heart transplant!

> Ezekiel 36:26 A new heart also will I give you, and a new spirit will I put within you: and I will take away the stony heart out of your flesh, and I will give you an heart of flesh.

The new healed heart is now in tune with God. It is able to contain God's love and peace. All of those tormenting emotions now can be permanently ended as we are set free to live with God's peace in our hearts. Through the mighty power of the Holy Spirit, God now can put to death fear, anxiety, and depression, which torment so many people.

> 2Timothy 1:7 For God hath not given us the spirit of fear; but of power, and of love, and of a sound mind.

God has designed the healed heart to contain His love and peace. As we grow in God, His love and peace grows in us, to the point that nothing can take away God's peace and nothing can drain His love from our hearts. God sent

Jesus Christ to heal the brokenhearted so we can live with God in the fullness of His love and peace!

The first step in healing a broken heart is to believe the gospel of Jesus Christ. Before God can heal the brokenhearted, the penalty for sin must be addressed. The next step involves forgiveness. This forgiveness might involve yourself or another person such as a parent. It might even involve reconciling with God. Through Jesus Christ, God forgives all of our sins, and He requires that we forgive everyone who has sinned against us and broken our hearts.

> Matthew 6:14 For if ye forgive men their trespasses, your heavenly Father will also forgive you:

If someone feels the event that broke his heart was so severe that it cannot be forgiven, then that person has to turn to God and ask for God's grace and love so he can forgive. God will give whatever is needed for you to accomplish this.

This forgiveness also includes yourself, since some people have committed sins that they feel God will not forgive. They may have a strong dislike for themselves. This is especially true of a woman who has had an abortion. If the woman repents of this and turns to Jesus Christ as her Savior, then God completely forgives her. But she must accept His forgiveness to have her heart healed. We need to live with God's view of us rather than with the view that was driven into us through a lifetime of sin.

Other people have a grudge against God for some reason but this too must be confessed to God for them to have their hearts healed. Once a person forgives whatever has broken their heart, God is free to heal that heart and set the person free.

Healing the brokenhearted is extremely important to God. It is not a minor issue with Him but ranks in importance right after Jesus Christ's gospel of eternal salvation. Through faith in Jesus Christ, God has provided all that we need to live with a healed heart that is full of God's love, peace and joy.

God as Abba Father

Romans 8:15 ... ye have received the Spirit of adoption, whereby we cry, Abba, Father.

What is truly amazing is that the Creator of the universe wants a relationship with you as your Abba, Daddy, Father! The word "abba" is the Hebrew word for "daddy". Once a person is free from the penalty of sin and has a healed heart, God desires a special relationship with him.

This relationship is not merely as father, but as abba. There is a huge difference between the relationship of a father and child when the child is 30, and between a father and youngster who is 6 years old. At 30, a son is expected to be independent and on his own. He is expected both to provide for himself and to defend himself. But at 6, a child expects his abba to provide for him and to protect him.

This is the special relationship that God wants with you, not just as your Father, but as your Abba. With God as your Abba, you can completely trust Him both to protect and provide for you in all areas of your life. You are not on your own, but you are secure with Abba. God wants you to feel safe with Him.

Unfortunately, many today grow up without a loving, earthly abba father, and therefore, it is difficult for them to see God as their Abba Father. The relationship we develop with a human father carries over to the way we see God.

If someone grew up with an abusive father, it is probable he will see God that way also. If you were raised without a father, or with a father who rejected you, then God can seem just as uncaring and distant. We really do see God in the way that we were raised as children. That is why it is so important for parents to raise their children with love and acceptance.

As you commit your life to God through Jesus Christ, He will reveal Himself to you as Abba Father. God desires to live this way with you. It may take time, but as you stay faithful to God through His word, He will live with you as Abba Father.

> Galatians 4:6 And because ye are sons, God hath sent forth the Spirit of his Son into your hearts, crying, Abba, Father. (7) Wherefore thou art no more a servant, but a son; and if a son, then an heir of God through Christ.

If you did not say the earlier prayer to confess Jesus Christ as your Savior, now is the time. It is also the time to ask God to heal your broken heart so you can live with Him as Abba Father. Now is the time to come to God with a prayer such as this:

> God, I confess my sin to you and repent of it. I believe that Jesus Christ died on the cross and shed His blood for my sin. I want Him as my Advocate, so I can be freed from the penalty of sin. I now confess Jesus Christ as my Lord and Savior and I

realize that I now have eternal life with you as my Abba Father.

Father God I ask you to heal my broken heart. I forgive all who have broken my heart. Please heal it of fear, anxiety, terror, hate, depression, trauma, bitterness and rejection, and free me of drugs, alcohol and all addictions. Thank You for sending Jesus Christ to free me from sin and to heal my broken heart. I want to live with You as my Abba Father.

Now that you have confessed Jesus Christ as your Advocate and are living with God as your Abba Father, God has opened the prison doors so you are no longer bound. You are free from the penalty of sin and now have eternal life with God. With a healed heart, the internal prison doors are open, and you are no longer bound and imprisoned by sin.

If the Son therefore shall make you free, ye shall be free indeed. John 8:36